Smart 2 Journal

MEDITATION JOURNAL
JOURNAL IS THE KEY FOR SUCCESS

Published by PUBLISHING COMPANY in 2016

First edition: First printing

Illustrations and design © 2016 author name

This Book Belong To :

ISBN-13: 978-1984015327
ISBN-10: 198401532X

DATE: /   /   TIME: -

PLACE: _____

I WILL ACCOMPLISH THESE THINGS TODAY

1._____

2._____

3._____

MY MEDITATION'S INTENSION FOR TODAY ARE

_____

_____

_____

_____

_____

_____

_____

_____

_____

_____

_____

_____

THOUGHTS AFTER MEDITATION _____

_____

_____

_____

_____

_____

_____

_____

_____

_____

_____

_____

_____

_____

I'M THANKFUL FOR _____

_____

_____

_____

_____

_____

DATE: /   /   TIME: -

PLACE: _____

I WILL ACCOMPLISH THESE THINGS TODAY

1._____

2._____

3._____

MY MEDITATION'S INTENSION FOR TODAY ARE

_____

_____

_____

_____

_____

_____

_____

_____

_____

_____

_____

_____

_____

_____

THOUGHTS AFTER MEDITATION _____

_____

_____

_____

_____

_____

_____

_____

_____

_____

_____

_____

_____

_____

I'M THANKFUL FOR _____

_____

_____

_____

_____

_____

DATE: /   /   TIME: -

PLACE: _____

I WILL ACCOMPLISH THESE THINGS TODAY

1._____

2._____

3._____

MY MEDITATION'S INTENSION FOR TODAY ARE

_____

_____

_____

_____

_____

_____

_____

_____

_____

_____

_____

_____

_____

THOUGHTS AFTER MEDITATION _____

_____

_____

_____

_____

_____

_____

_____

_____

_____

_____

_____

_____

_____

I'M THANKFUL FOR _____

_____

_____

_____

_____

_____

DATE: /   /   TIME: -

PLACE: _____

I WILL ACCOMPLISH THESE THINGS TODAY

1._____

2._____

3._____

MY MEDITATION'S INTENSION FOR TODAY ARE

_____

_____

_____

_____

_____

_____

_____

_____

_____

_____

_____

_____

_____

THOUGHTS AFTER MEDITATION _____

_____

_____

_____

_____

_____

_____

_____

_____

_____

_____

_____

_____

_____

I'M THANKFUL FOR _____

_____

_____

_____

_____

_____

DATE: /   /   TIME: -

PLACE: _____

I WILL ACCOMPLISH THESE THINGS TODAY

1._____

2._____

3._____

MY MEDITATION'S INTENSION FOR TODAY ARE

_____

_____

_____

_____

_____

_____

_____

_____

_____

_____

_____

_____

_____

_____

THOUGHTS AFTER MEDITATION _____

_____

_____

_____

_____

_____

_____

_____

_____

_____

_____

_____

_____

I'M THANKFUL FOR _____

_____

_____

_____

_____

_____

DATE: /   /   TIME: -

PLACE: _____

I WILL ACCOMPLISH THESE THINGS TODAY

1._____

2._____

3._____

MY MEDITATION'S INTENSION FOR TODAY ARE

_____

_____

_____

_____

_____

_____

_____

_____

_____

_____

_____

_____

_____

_____

THOUGHTS AFTER MEDITATION _____

_____

_____

_____

_____

_____

_____

_____

_____

_____

_____

_____

_____

I'M THANKFUL FOR _____

_____

_____

_____

_____

_____

DATE: /   /   TIME: -

PLACE: _____

I WILL ACCOMPLISH THESE THINGS TODAY

1._____

2._____

3._____

MY MEDITATION'S INTENSION FOR TODAY ARE

_____

_____

_____

_____

_____

_____

_____

_____

_____

_____

_____

_____

THOUGHTS AFTER MEDITATION _____

_____

_____

_____

_____

_____

_____

_____

_____

_____

_____

_____

_____

_____

I'M THANKFUL FOR _____

_____

_____

_____

_____

_____

DATE: /   /   TIME: -

PLACE: _____

I WILL ACCOMPLISH THESE THINGS TODAY

1._____

2._____

3._____

MY MEDITATION'S INTENSION FOR TODAY ARE

_____

_____

_____

_____

_____

_____

_____

_____

_____

_____

_____

_____

_____

THOUGHTS AFTER MEDITATION _____

_____

_____

_____

_____

_____

_____

_____

_____

_____

_____

_____

_____

_____

_____

I'M THANKFUL FOR _____

_____

_____

_____

_____

_____

DATE: /   /   TIME: -

PLACE: _____

I WILL ACCOMPLISH THESE THINGS TODAY

1._____

2._____

3._____

MY MEDITATION'S INTENSION FOR TODAY ARE

_____

_____

_____

_____

_____

_____

_____

_____

_____

_____

_____

_____

_____

_____

THOUGHTS AFTER MEDITATION _____

_____

_____

_____

_____

_____

_____

_____

_____

_____

_____

_____

_____

_____

I'M THANKFUL FOR _____

_____

_____

_____

_____

DATE: / / TIME: -

PLACE: _____

I WILL ACCOMPLISH THESE THINGS TODAY

1._____

2._____

3._____

MY MEDITATION'S INTENSION FOR TODAY ARE

_____

_____

_____

_____

_____

_____

_____

_____

_____

_____

_____

_____

_____

THOUGHTS AFTER MEDITATION _____

_____

_____

_____

_____

_____

_____

_____

_____

_____

_____

_____

_____

_____

I'M THANKFUL FOR _____

_____

_____

_____

_____

_____

DATE: /   /   TIME: -

PLACE: _____

I WILL ACCOMPLISH THESE THINGS TODAY

1._____

2._____

3._____

MY MEDITATION'S INTENSION FOR TODAY ARE

_____

_____

_____

_____

_____

_____

_____

_____

_____

_____

_____

_____

_____

THOUGHTS AFTER MEDITATION _____

_____

_____

_____

_____

_____

_____

_____

_____

_____

_____

_____

_____

_____

_____

I'M THANKFUL FOR _____

_____

_____

_____

_____

_____

DATE: /   /   TIME: -

PLACE: _____

I WILL ACCOMPLISH THESE THINGS TODAY

1._____

2._____

3._____

MY MEDITATION'S INTENSION FOR TODAY ARE

_____

_____

_____

_____

_____

_____

_____

_____

_____

_____

_____

_____

_____

THOUGHTS AFTER MEDITATION _____

_____

_____

_____

_____

_____

_____

_____

_____

_____

_____

_____

_____

_____

I'M THANKFUL FOR _____

_____

_____

_____

_____

_____

DATE: /   /   TIME: -

PLACE: _____

I WILL ACCOMPLISH THESE THINGS TODAY

1._____

2._____

3._____

MY MEDITATION'S INTENSION FOR TODAY ARE

_____

_____

_____

_____

_____

_____

_____

_____

_____

_____

_____

_____

_____

THOUGHTS AFTER MEDITATION _____

_____

_____

_____

_____

_____

_____

_____

_____

_____

_____

_____

_____

_____

I'M THANKFUL FOR _____

_____

_____

_____

_____

_____

DATE: /   /   TIME: -

PLACE: _____

I WILL ACCOMPLISH THESE THINGS TODAY

1._____

2._____

3._____

MY MEDITATION'S INTENSION FOR TODAY ARE

_____

_____

_____

_____

_____

_____

_____

_____

_____

_____

_____

_____

_____

THOUGHTS AFTER MEDITATION _____

_____

_____

_____

_____

_____

_____

_____

_____

_____

_____

_____

_____

_____

I'M THANKFUL FOR _____

_____

_____

_____

_____

_____

DATE: /   /   TIME: -

PLACE: _____

I WILL ACCOMPLISH THESE THINGS TODAY

1._____

2._____

3._____

MY MEDITATION'S INTENSION FOR TODAY ARE

_____

_____

_____

_____

_____

_____

_____

_____

_____

_____

_____

_____

THOUGHTS AFTER MEDITATION _____

_____

_____

_____

_____

_____

_____

_____

_____

_____

_____

_____

_____

_____

_____

I'M THANKFUL FOR _____

_____

_____

_____

_____

_____

DATE: /   /   TIME: -

PLACE: _____

I WILL ACCOMPLISH THESE THINGS TODAY

1._____

2._____

3._____

MY MEDITATION'S INTENSION FOR TODAY ARE

_____

_____

_____

_____

_____

_____

_____

_____

_____

_____

_____

_____

THOUGHTS AFTER MEDITATION _____

_____

_____

_____

_____

_____

_____

_____

_____

_____

_____

_____

_____

_____

I'M THANKFUL FOR _____

_____

_____

_____

_____

_____

DATE: /   /   TIME: -

PLACE: _____

I WILL ACCOMPLISH THESE THINGS TODAY

1._____

2._____

3._____

MY MEDITATION'S INTENSION FOR TODAY ARE

_____

_____

_____

_____

_____

_____

_____

_____

_____

_____

_____

_____

_____

THOUGHTS AFTER MEDITATION _____

_____

_____

_____

_____

_____

_____

_____

_____

_____

_____

_____

_____

_____

_____

I'M THANKFUL FOR _____

_____

_____

_____

_____

_____

DATE: /   /   TIME: -

PLACE: _____

I WILL ACCOMPLISH THESE THINGS TODAY

1._____

2._____

3._____

MY MEDITATION'S INTENSION FOR TODAY ARE

_____

_____

_____

_____

_____

_____

_____

_____

_____

_____

_____

_____

THOUGHTS AFTER MEDITATION _____

_____

_____

_____

_____

_____

_____

_____

_____

_____

_____

_____

_____

_____

I'M THANKFUL FOR _____

_____

_____

_____

_____

_____

DATE: /   /   TIME: -

PLACE: _____

I WILL ACCOMPLISH THESE THINGS TODAY

1._____

2._____

3._____

MY MEDITATION'S INTENSION FOR TODAY ARE

_____

_____

_____

_____

_____

_____

_____

_____

_____

_____

_____

_____

_____

THOUGHTS AFTER MEDITATION _____

_____

_____

_____

_____

_____

_____

_____

_____

_____

_____

_____

_____

_____

_____

I'M THANKFUL FOR _____

_____

_____

_____

_____

_____

DATE: /   /   TIME: -

PLACE: _____

I WILL ACCOMPLISH THESE THINGS TODAY

1._____

2._____

3._____

MY MEDITATION'S INTENSION FOR TODAY ARE

_____

_____

_____

_____

_____

_____

_____

_____

_____

_____

_____

_____

THOUGHTS AFTER MEDITATION _____

_____

_____

_____

_____

_____

_____

_____

_____

_____

_____

_____

_____

_____

_____

_____

I'M THANKFUL FOR _____

_____

_____

_____

_____

_____

DATE: /   /   TIME: -

PLACE: _____

I WILL ACCOMPLISH THESE THINGS TODAY

1._____

2._____

3._____

MY MEDITATION'S INTENSION FOR TODAY ARE

_____

_____

_____

_____

_____

_____

_____

_____

_____

_____

_____

_____

_____

THOUGHTS AFTER MEDITATION _____

_____

_____

_____

_____

_____

_____

_____

_____

_____

_____

_____

_____

I'M THANKFUL FOR _____

_____

_____

_____

_____

_____

DATE: /   /   TIME: -

PLACE: _____

I WILL ACCOMPLISH THESE THINGS TODAY

1._____

2._____

3._____

MY MEDITATION'S INTENSION FOR TODAY ARE

_____

_____

_____

_____

_____

_____

_____

_____

_____

_____

_____

_____

_____

THOUGHTS AFTER MEDITATION _____

_____

_____

_____

_____

_____

_____

_____

_____

_____

_____

_____

_____

_____

I'M THANKFUL FOR _____

_____

_____

_____

_____

_____

DATE: /   /   TIME: -

PLACE: _____

I WILL ACCOMPLISH THESE THINGS TODAY

1._____

2._____

3._____

MY MEDITATION'S INTENSION FOR TODAY ARE

_____

_____

_____

_____

_____

_____

_____

_____

_____

_____

_____

_____

THOUGHTS AFTER MEDITATION _____

_____

_____

_____

_____

_____

_____

_____

_____

_____

_____

_____

_____

I'M THANKFUL FOR _____

_____

_____

_____

_____

_____

DATE: /   /   TIME: -

PLACE: _____

I WILL ACCOMPLISH THESE THINGS TODAY

1._____

2._____

3._____

MY MEDITATION'S INTENSION FOR TODAY ARE

_____

_____

_____

_____

_____

_____

_____

_____

_____

_____

_____

_____

_____

THOUGHTS AFTER MEDITATION _____

_____

_____

_____

_____

_____

_____

_____

_____

_____

_____

_____

_____

_____

I'M THANKFUL FOR _____

_____

_____

_____

_____

_____

DATE: /   /   TIME: -

PLACE: _____

I WILL ACCOMPLISH THESE THINGS TODAY

1._____

2._____

3._____

MY MEDITATION'S INTENSION FOR TODAY ARE

_____

_____

_____

_____

_____

_____

_____

_____

_____

_____

_____

_____

_____

_____

THOUGHTS AFTER MEDITATION _____

_____

_____

_____

_____

_____

_____

_____

_____

_____

_____

_____

_____

_____

_____

I'M THANKFUL FOR _____

_____

_____

_____

_____

_____

DATE: /   /   TIME: -

PLACE: _____

I WILL ACCOMPLISH THESE THINGS TODAY

1._____

2._____

3._____

MY MEDITATION'S INTENSION FOR TODAY ARE

_____

_____

_____

_____

_____

_____

_____

_____

_____

_____

_____

_____

_____

THOUGHTS AFTER MEDITATION _____

_____

_____

_____

_____

_____

_____

_____

_____

_____

_____

_____

_____

_____

I'M THANKFUL FOR _____

_____

_____

_____

_____

_____

DATE: /   /   TIME: -

PLACE: _____

I WILL ACCOMPLISH THESE THINGS TODAY

1._____

2._____

3._____

MY MEDITATION'S INTENSION FOR TODAY ARE

_____

_____

_____

_____

_____

_____

_____

_____

_____

_____

_____

_____

_____

THOUGHTS AFTER MEDITATION _____

_____

_____

_____

_____

_____

_____

_____

_____

_____

_____

_____

_____

_____

I'M THANKFUL FOR _____

_____

_____

_____

_____

_____

DATE: /   /   TIME: -

PLACE: _____

I WILL ACCOMPLISH THESE THINGS TODAY

1._____

2._____

3._____

MY MEDITATION'S INTENSION FOR TODAY ARE

_____

_____

_____

_____

_____

_____

_____

_____

_____

_____

_____

_____

_____

THOUGHTS AFTER MEDITATION _____

_____

_____

_____

_____

_____

_____

_____

_____

_____

_____

_____

_____

_____

I'M THANKFUL FOR _____

_____

_____

_____

_____

_____

DATE: /   /   TIME: -

PLACE: _____

I WILL ACCOMPLISH THESE THINGS TODAY

1._____

2._____

3._____

MY MEDITATION'S INTENSION FOR TODAY ARE

_____

_____

_____

_____

_____

_____

_____

_____

_____

_____

_____

_____

THOUGHTS AFTER MEDITATION _____

_____

_____

_____

_____

_____

_____

_____

_____

_____

_____

_____

_____

I'M THANKFUL FOR _____

_____

_____

_____

_____

_____

DATE: /   /   TIME: -

PLACE: _____

I WILL ACCOMPLISH THESE THINGS TODAY

1._____

2._____

3._____

MY MEDITATION'S INTENSION FOR TODAY ARE

_____

_____

_____

_____

_____

_____

_____

_____

_____

_____

_____

_____

_____

_____

THOUGHTS AFTER MEDITATION _____

_____

_____

_____

_____

_____

_____

_____

_____

_____

_____

_____

_____

_____

_____

I'M THANKFUL FOR _____

_____

_____

_____

_____

_____

DATE: /   /   TIME: -

PLACE: _____

I WILL ACCOMPLISH THESE THINGS TODAY

1._____

2._____

3._____

MY MEDITATION'S INTENSION FOR TODAY ARE

_____

_____

_____

_____

_____

_____

_____

_____

_____

_____

_____

_____

THOUGHTS AFTER MEDITATION _____

_____

_____

_____

_____

_____

_____

_____

_____

_____

_____

_____

_____

I'M THANKFUL FOR _____

_____

_____

_____

_____

_____

DATE: /   /   TIME: -

PLACE: _____

I WILL ACCOMPLISH THESE THINGS TODAY

1._____

2._____

3._____

MY MEDITATION'S INTENSION FOR TODAY ARE

_____

_____

_____

_____

_____

_____

_____

_____

_____

_____

_____

_____

THOUGHTS AFTER MEDITATION _____

_____

_____

_____

_____

_____

_____

_____

_____

_____

_____

_____

_____

_____

I'M THANKFUL FOR _____

_____

_____

_____

_____

_____

DATE: /   /   TIME: -

PLACE: _____

I WILL ACCOMPLISH THESE THINGS TODAY

1._____

2._____

3._____

MY MEDITATION'S INTENSION FOR TODAY ARE

_____

_____

_____

_____

_____

_____

_____

_____

_____

_____

_____

_____

_____

THOUGHTS AFTER MEDITATION _____

_____

_____

_____

_____

_____

_____

_____

_____

_____

_____

_____

_____

_____

I'M THANKFUL FOR _____

_____

_____

_____

_____

_____

DATE: /   /   TIME: -

PLACE: _____

I WILL ACCOMPLISH THESE THINGS TODAY

1._____

2._____

3._____

MY MEDITATION'S INTENSION FOR TODAY ARE

_____

_____

_____

_____

_____

_____

_____

_____

_____

_____

_____

_____

_____

THOUGHTS AFTER MEDITATION _____

_____

_____

_____

_____

_____

_____

_____

_____

_____

_____

_____

_____

_____

_____

I'M THANKFUL FOR _____

_____

_____

_____

_____

_____

DATE: /   /   TIME: -

PLACE: _____

I WILL ACCOMPLISH THESE THINGS TODAY

1._____

2._____

3._____

MY MEDITATION'S INTENSION FOR TODAY ARE

_____

_____

_____

_____

_____

_____

_____

_____

_____

_____

_____

_____

_____

THOUGHTS AFTER MEDITATION _____

_____

_____

_____

_____

_____

_____

_____

_____

_____

_____

_____

I'M THANKFUL FOR _____

_____

_____

_____

_____

_____

DATE: /   /   TIME: -

PLACE: _____

I WILL ACCOMPLISH THESE THINGS TODAY

1._____

2._____

3._____

MY MEDITATION'S INTENSION FOR TODAY ARE

_____

_____

_____

_____

_____

_____

_____

_____

_____

_____

_____

_____

_____

THOUGHTS AFTER MEDITATION _____

_____

_____

_____

_____

_____

_____

_____

_____

_____

_____

_____

_____

_____

I'M THANKFUL FOR _____

_____

_____

_____

_____

_____

DATE: /   /   TIME: -

PLACE: _____

I WILL ACCOMPLISH THESE THINGS TODAY

1._____

2._____

3._____

MY MEDITATION'S INTENSION FOR TODAY ARE

_____

_____

_____

_____

_____

_____

_____

_____

_____

_____

_____

_____

_____

_____

THOUGHTS AFTER MEDITATION _____

_____

_____

_____

_____

_____

_____

_____

_____

_____

_____

_____

I'M THANKFUL FOR _____

_____

_____

_____

_____

DATE: /   /   TIME: -

PLACE: _____

I WILL ACCOMPLISH THESE THINGS TODAY

1._____

2._____

3._____

MY MEDITATION'S INTENSION FOR TODAY ARE

_____

_____

_____

_____

_____

_____

_____

_____

_____

_____

_____

_____

_____

_____

THOUGHTS AFTER MEDITATION _____

_____

_____

_____

_____

_____

_____

_____

_____

_____

_____

_____

_____

_____

I'M THANKFUL FOR _____

_____

_____

_____

_____

_____

DATE: /   /   TIME: -

PLACE: _____

I WILL ACCOMPLISH THESE THINGS TODAY

1._____

2._____

3._____

MY MEDITATION'S INTENSION FOR TODAY ARE

_____

_____

_____

_____

_____

_____

_____

_____

_____

_____

_____

_____

_____

THOUGHTS AFTER MEDITATION _____

_____

_____

_____

_____

_____

_____

_____

_____

_____

_____

_____

_____

_____

I'M THANKFUL FOR _____

_____

_____

_____

_____

_____

DATE: /   /   TIME: -

PLACE: _____

I WILL ACCOMPLISH THESE THINGS TODAY

1._____

2._____

3._____

MY MEDITATION'S INTENSION FOR TODAY ARE

_____

_____

_____

_____

_____

_____

_____

_____

_____

_____

_____

_____

_____

_____

THOUGHTS AFTER MEDITATION _____

_____

_____

_____

_____

_____

_____

_____

_____

_____

_____

_____

_____

I'M THANKFUL FOR _____

_____

_____

_____

_____

_____

DATE: /   /   TIME: -

PLACE: _____

I WILL ACCOMPLISH THESE THINGS TODAY

1._____

2._____

3._____

MY MEDITATION'S INTENSION FOR TODAY ARE

_____

_____

_____

_____

_____

_____

_____

_____

_____

_____

_____

_____

_____

THOUGHTS AFTER MEDITATION _____

_____

_____

_____

_____

_____

_____

_____

_____

_____

_____

_____

_____

_____

I'M THANKFUL FOR _____

_____

_____

_____

_____

_____

DATE: /   /   TIME: -

PLACE: _____

I WILL ACCOMPLISH THESE THINGS TODAY

1._____

2._____

3._____

MY MEDITATION'S INTENSION FOR TODAY ARE

_____

_____

_____

_____

_____

_____

_____

_____

_____

_____

_____

_____

_____

THOUGHTS AFTER MEDITATION _____

_____

_____

_____

_____

_____

_____

_____

_____

_____

_____

_____

_____

_____

I'M THANKFUL FOR _____

_____

_____

_____

_____

_____

DATE: /   /   TIME: -

PLACE: _____

I WILL ACCOMPLISH THESE THINGS TODAY

1._____

2._____

3._____

MY MEDITATION'S INTENSION FOR TODAY ARE

_____

_____

_____

_____

_____

_____

_____

_____

_____

_____

_____

_____

_____

THOUGHTS AFTER MEDITATION _____

_____

_____

_____

_____

_____

_____

_____

_____

_____

_____

_____

_____

_____

I'M THANKFUL FOR _____

_____

_____

_____

_____

_____

DATE: /   /   TIME: -

PLACE: _____

I WILL ACCOMPLISH THESE THINGS TODAY

1._____

2._____

3._____

MY MEDITATION'S INTENSION FOR TODAY ARE

_____

_____

_____

_____

_____

_____

_____

_____

_____

_____

_____

_____

_____

THOUGHTS AFTER MEDITATION _____

_____

_____

_____

_____

_____

_____

_____

_____

_____

_____

_____

_____

_____

I'M THANKFUL FOR _____

_____

_____

_____

_____

_____

DATE: /   /   TIME: -

PLACE: _____

I WILL ACCOMPLISH THESE THINGS TODAY

1._____

2._____

3._____

MY MEDITATION'S INTENSION FOR TODAY ARE

_____

_____

_____

_____

_____

_____

_____

_____

_____

_____

_____

_____

THOUGHTS AFTER MEDITATION _____

_____

_____

_____

_____

_____

_____

_____

_____

_____

_____

_____

_____

I'M THANKFUL FOR _____

_____

_____

_____

_____

_____

DATE: /   /   TIME: -

PLACE: _____

I WILL ACCOMPLISH THESE THINGS TODAY

1._____

2._____

3._____

MY MEDITATION'S INTENSION FOR TODAY ARE

_____

_____

_____

_____

_____

_____

_____

_____

_____

_____

_____

_____

THOUGHTS AFTER MEDITATION _____

_____

_____

_____

_____

_____

_____

_____

_____

_____

_____

_____

_____

I'M THANKFUL FOR _____

_____

_____

_____

_____

_____

DATE: /   /   TIME: -

PLACE: _____

I WILL ACCOMPLISH THESE THINGS TODAY

1._____

2._____

3._____

MY MEDITATION'S INTENSION FOR TODAY ARE

_____

_____

_____

_____

_____

_____

_____

_____

_____

_____

_____

_____

_____

_____

THOUGHTS AFTER MEDITATION _____

_____

_____

_____

_____

_____

_____

_____

_____

_____

_____

_____

_____

I'M THANKFUL FOR _____

_____

_____

_____

_____

_____

DATE: /   /   TIME: -

PLACE: _____

I WILL ACCOMPLISH THESE THINGS TODAY

1._____

2._____

3._____

MY MEDITATION'S INTENSION FOR TODAY ARE

_____

_____

_____

_____

_____

_____

_____

_____

_____

_____

_____

_____

_____

_____

THOUGHTS AFTER MEDITATION _____

_____

_____

_____

_____

_____

_____

_____

_____

_____

_____

_____

_____

_____

I'M THANKFUL FOR _____

_____

_____

_____

_____

_____

DATE: / / TIME: -

PLACE: _____

I WILL ACCOMPLISH THESE THINGS TODAY

1._____

2._____

3._____

MY MEDITATION'S INTENSION FOR TODAY ARE

_____

_____

_____

_____

_____

_____

_____

_____

_____

_____

_____

_____

_____

THOUGHTS AFTER MEDITATION _____

_____

_____

_____

_____

_____

_____

_____

_____

_____

_____

_____

_____

I'M THANKFUL FOR _____

_____

_____

_____

_____

_____

DATE: /   /   TIME: -

PLACE: _____

I WILL ACCOMPLISH THESE THINGS TODAY

1._____

2._____

3._____

MY MEDITATION'S INTENSION FOR TODAY ARE

_____

_____

_____

_____

_____

_____

_____

_____

_____

_____

_____

_____

_____

THOUGHTS AFTER MEDITATION _____

_____

_____

_____

_____

_____

_____

_____

_____

_____

_____

_____

I'M THANKFUL FOR _____

_____

_____

_____

_____

DATE: /   /   TIME: -

PLACE: _____

I WILL ACCOMPLISH THESE THINGS TODAY

1._____

2._____

3._____

MY MEDITATION'S INTENSION FOR TODAY ARE

_____

_____

_____

_____

_____

_____

_____

_____

_____

_____

_____

_____

_____

_____

THOUGHTS AFTER MEDITATION _____

_____

_____

_____

_____

_____

_____

_____

_____

_____

_____

_____

I'M THANKFUL FOR _____

_____

_____

_____

_____

_____

DATE: /   /   TIME: -

PLACE: _____

I WILL ACCOMPLISH THESE THINGS TODAY

1._____

2._____

3._____

MY MEDITATION'S INTENSION FOR TODAY ARE

_____

_____

_____

_____

_____

_____

_____

_____

_____

_____

_____

_____

_____

_____

_____

THOUGHTS AFTER MEDITATION _____

_____

_____

_____

_____

_____

_____

_____

_____

_____

_____

_____

_____

_____

I'M THANKFUL FOR _____

_____

_____

_____

_____

_____

DATE: /   /   TIME: -
PLACE: _____

I WILL ACCOMPLISH THESE THINGS TODAY

1._____

2._____

3._____

MY MEDITATION'S INTENSION FOR TODAY ARE

_____

_____

_____

_____

_____

_____

_____

_____

_____

_____

_____

_____

_____

THOUGHTS AFTER MEDITATION _____

_____

_____

_____

_____

_____

_____

_____

_____

_____

_____

_____

_____

_____

I'M THANKFUL FOR _____

_____

_____

_____

_____

_____

DATE: /   /   TIME: -

PLACE: _____

I WILL ACCOMPLISH THESE THINGS TODAY

1._____

2._____

3._____

MY MEDITATION'S INTENSION FOR TODAY ARE

_____

_____

_____

_____

_____

_____

_____

_____

_____

_____

_____

_____

_____

THOUGHTS AFTER MEDITATION _____

_____

_____

_____

_____

_____

_____

_____

_____

_____

_____

_____

_____

_____

I'M THANKFUL FOR _____

_____

_____

_____

_____

_____

DATE: /   /   TIME: -

PLACE: _____

I WILL ACCOMPLISH THESE THINGS TODAY

1._____

2._____

3._____

MY MEDITATION'S INTENSION FOR TODAY ARE

_____

_____

_____

_____

_____

_____

_____

_____

_____

_____

_____

_____

_____

THOUGHTS AFTER MEDITATION _____

_____

_____

_____

_____

_____

_____

_____

_____

_____

_____

_____

_____

_____

I'M THANKFUL FOR _____

_____

_____

_____

_____

_____

DATE: /   /   TIME: -

PLACE: _____

I WILL ACCOMPLISH THESE THINGS TODAY

1._____

2._____

3._____

MY MEDITATION'S INTENSION FOR TODAY ARE

_____

_____

_____

_____

_____

_____

_____

_____

_____

_____

_____

_____

_____

THOUGHTS AFTER MEDITATION _____

_____

_____

_____

_____

_____

_____

_____

_____

_____

_____

_____

_____

_____

I'M THANKFUL FOR _____

_____

_____

_____

_____

_____

DATE: /   /   TIME: -

PLACE: _____

I WILL ACCOMPLISH THESE THINGS TODAY

1._____

2._____

3._____

MY MEDITATION'S INTENSION FOR TODAY ARE

_____

_____

_____

_____

_____

_____

_____

_____

_____

_____

_____

_____

_____

THOUGHTS AFTER MEDITATION _____

_____

_____

_____

_____

_____

_____

_____

_____

_____

_____

_____

_____

I'M THANKFUL FOR _____

_____

_____

_____

_____

_____

DATE: /   /   TIME: -

PLACE: _____

I WILL ACCOMPLISH THESE THINGS TODAY

1._____

2._____

3._____

MY MEDITATION'S INTENSION FOR TODAY ARE

_____

_____

_____

_____

_____

_____

_____

_____

_____

_____

_____

_____

_____

THOUGHTS AFTER MEDITATION _____

_____

_____

_____

_____

_____

_____

_____

_____

_____

_____

_____

I'M THANKFUL FOR _____

_____

_____

_____

_____

_____

DATE: /   /   TIME: -

PLACE: _____

I WILL ACCOMPLISH THESE THINGS TODAY

1._____

2._____

3._____

MY MEDITATION'S INTENSION FOR TODAY ARE

_____

_____

_____

_____

_____

_____

_____

_____

_____

_____

_____

_____

THOUGHTS AFTER MEDITATION _____

_____

_____

_____

_____

_____

_____

_____

_____

_____

_____

_____

_____

_____

I'M THANKFUL FOR _____

_____

_____

_____

_____

_____

DATE: /   /   TIME: -

PLACE: _____

I WILL ACCOMPLISH THESE THINGS TODAY

1._____

2._____

3._____

MY MEDITATION'S INTENSION FOR TODAY ARE

_____

_____

_____

_____

_____

_____

_____

_____

_____

_____

_____

_____

_____

THOUGHTS AFTER MEDITATION _____

_____

_____

_____

_____

_____

_____

_____

_____

_____

_____

_____

_____

_____

I'M THANKFUL FOR _____

_____

_____

_____

_____

_____

DATE: /   /   TIME: -

PLACE: _____

I WILL ACCOMPLISH THESE THINGS TODAY

1._____

2._____

3._____

MY MEDITATION'S INTENSION FOR TODAY ARE

_____

_____

_____

_____

_____

_____

_____

_____

_____

_____

_____

_____

_____

THOUGHTS AFTER MEDITATION _____

_____

_____

_____

_____

_____

_____

_____

_____

_____

_____

_____

_____

I'M THANKFUL FOR _____

_____

_____

_____

_____

_____

DATE: /   /   TIME: -

PLACE: _____

I WILL ACCOMPLISH THESE THINGS TODAY

1._____

2._____

3._____

MY MEDITATION'S INTENSION FOR TODAY ARE

_____

_____

_____

_____

_____

_____

_____

_____

_____

_____

_____

_____

THOUGHTS AFTER MEDITATION _____

_____

_____

_____

_____

_____

_____

_____

_____

_____

_____

_____

_____

_____

I'M THANKFUL FOR _____

_____

_____

_____

_____

_____

DATE: / / TIME: -

PLACE: _____

I WILL ACCOMPLISH THESE THINGS TODAY

1._____

2._____

3._____

MY MEDITATION'S INTENSION FOR TODAY ARE

_____

_____

_____

_____

_____

_____

_____

_____

_____

_____

_____

_____

_____

_____

THOUGHTS AFTER MEDITATION _____

_____

_____

_____

_____

_____

_____

_____

_____

_____

_____

_____

_____

_____

I'M THANKFUL FOR _____

_____

_____

_____

_____

_____

DATE: / / TIME: -

PLACE: _____

I WILL ACCOMPLISH THESE THINGS TODAY

1._____

2._____

3._____

MY MEDITATION'S INTENSION FOR TODAY ARE

_____

_____

_____

_____

_____

_____

_____

_____

_____

_____

_____

_____

THOUGHTS AFTER MEDITATION _____

_____

_____

_____

_____

_____

_____

_____

_____

_____

_____

_____

_____

_____

I'M THANKFUL FOR _____

_____

_____

_____

_____

_____

DATE: /   /   TIME: -

PLACE: _____

I WILL ACCOMPLISH THESE THINGS TODAY

1._____

2._____

3._____

MY MEDITATION'S INTENSION FOR TODAY ARE

_____

_____

_____

_____

_____

_____

_____

_____

_____

_____

_____

_____

_____

THOUGHTS AFTER MEDITATION _____

_____

_____

_____

_____

_____

_____

_____

_____

_____

_____

_____

_____

I'M THANKFUL FOR _____

_____

_____

_____

_____

_____

DATE: /   /   TIME: -

PLACE: _____

I WILL ACCOMPLISH THESE THINGS TODAY

1._____

2._____

3._____

MY MEDITATION'S INTENSION FOR TODAY ARE

_____

_____

_____

_____

_____

_____

_____

_____

_____

_____

_____

_____

_____

THOUGHTS AFTER MEDITATION _____

_____

_____

_____

_____

_____

_____

_____

_____

_____

_____

_____

_____

_____

_____

I'M THANKFUL FOR _____

_____

_____

_____

_____

_____

DATE: / / TIME: -

PLACE: _____

I WILL ACCOMPLISH THESE THINGS TODAY

1._____

2._____

3._____

MY MEDITATION'S INTENSION FOR TODAY ARE

_____

_____

_____

_____

_____

_____

_____

_____

_____

_____

_____

_____

_____

THOUGHTS AFTER MEDITATION _____

_____

_____

_____

_____

_____

_____

_____

_____

_____

_____

_____

_____

_____

I'M THANKFUL FOR _____

_____

_____

_____

_____

_____

DATE: /   /   TIME: -

PLACE: _____

I WILL ACCOMPLISH THESE THINGS TODAY

1._____

2._____

3._____

MY MEDITATION'S INTENSION FOR TODAY ARE

_____

_____

_____

_____

_____

_____

_____

_____

_____

_____

_____

_____

_____

_____

_____

THOUGHTS AFTER MEDITATION _____

_____

_____

_____

_____

_____

_____

_____

_____

_____

_____

_____

_____

I'M THANKFUL FOR _____

_____

_____

_____

_____

_____

DATE: /   /   TIME: -

PLACE: _____

I WILL ACCOMPLISH THESE THINGS TODAY

1._____

2._____

3._____

MY MEDITATION'S INTENSION FOR TODAY ARE

_____

_____

_____

_____

_____

_____

_____

_____

_____

_____

_____

_____

_____

_____

THOUGHTS AFTER MEDITATION _____

_____

_____

_____

_____

_____

_____

_____

_____

_____

_____

_____

_____

I'M THANKFUL FOR _____

_____

_____

_____

_____

_____

DATE: /   /   TIME: -

PLACE: _____

I WILL ACCOMPLISH THESE THINGS TODAY

1._____

2._____

3._____

MY MEDITATION'S INTENSION FOR TODAY ARE

_____

_____

_____

_____

_____

_____

_____

_____

_____

_____

_____

_____

_____

THOUGHTS AFTER MEDITATION _____

_____

_____

_____

_____

_____

_____

_____

_____

_____

_____

_____

_____

I'M THANKFUL FOR _____

_____

_____

_____

_____

_____

93373531R00082

Made in the USA
Middletown, DE
13 October 2018